What's Eating Up Your Time?

The Full 24

J.R. Rivera

ISBN-13:
978-1978177581

ISBN-10:
1978177585

DEDICATION

To Jackie, my mother, my motivation, to my son, Kyrie, my biggest blessing, to my daughter Azariah, my inspiration, my brother Diamond, my sisters Toccara, and Krystal, to my grandmothers, Carmen and Josephine, my dad Wilfred Sr., to my Mile family and friends. And to all the students, athletes, and driven individuals anxiously awaiting the medication to kill procrastination

CONTENTS

ACKNOWLEDGMENTS

Where do I begin? So much work and effort go into a book like this. There are so many to thank. During the years I spent developing the ideas for "What's Eating Up Your Time," I benefited from the support of family, special friends, and mentors. Major credit can be given to the following: Phillip Buchanon, Dr. Eric Thomas, and my Extra Mile family for believing in a solution to procrastination and an unpublished writer. Because of their support and invaluable knowledge, I was eager to take the first step. To my Extra Mile family, thank you for waiting patiently for me to complete my journey of a thousand miles. To my students, for keeping me accountable and never allowing me to get lost in the daily battles of life. Again, a huge thank you to Phillip Buchanon who first believed and urged me to become a speaker as well as an author. To all the students at SLAM Miami Charter School who allowed me to perfect my gift as I worked to balance the job and the dream. And the last word goes to my source: my strength and faith in God that allowed me to achieve the impossible.

INTRO

How would you like to live twice as long, do twice as much, and of course enjoy accomplishing twice as much success in life?

According to the ancient Greek philosopher Theophrastus, **time** is "our costliest expenditure." **Time** must be used efficiently in order to accomplish all that needs to be done. **Time management theories** can help you understand what you are doing with the **time** in your life and how to improve effectiveness.

Manipulating the constraints which limit mankind sounds next to impossible, but if you're reading this book, I do know the following about you:

You believe in the impossible! (I'M possible)

If you have the time, in this book I will expose the power to stretch an hour. Focusing on three major components: Organization, Routine, and Urgency.

"Don't be fooled by the calendar. There are only as many days in the year as you make use of. One man gets only a week's value out of a year while another man gets a full year's value out of a week." —Charles Richards

1 VISION TO VALUE TIME

Time Value Chart

Hours	Minutes	Seconds
½	30	1,800
1	60	3,600
5	300	18,000

Average   Good   Great

The vision of a day is broken up into three categories: hours, minutes, and seconds. From my research, most average income people view time in hours; good income people view time in minutes, but the great income earners, the billionaires view the value of time in seconds.

You cannot begin to appreciate what you don't pay attention to. The first goal is to transition your thought of time into the next column.

Example:

If you're in the Average category, doing the 9-to-5, this may sound like a typical day: I have to go to school then work and do some home work. Realize there is no real attention to detail of the time in between the tasks.

While if you're in the Good category, this may sound like a typical day: I have to get some studying in before school starts, after school I will get my work clothes and stuff ready before I spend time writing the last two pages of my paper. Once I come from work, I will have time to talk to Facetime my good friend.

It takes time to change your values. In the great catergory the same persons day is blocked out. Blocked out means scheduling each important time frame of the day. This may sound like a typical day: I wake up at 5:30a.m. spend the first thirty minutes freshing up and the next thirty minutes on my breakfast and packing. On the thirty-minute car ride to school I will listen to my audio book about law. When I get to school I will have fifteen minutes to catch up with my friends. At lunch I will eat and study with my best friend fifteen minutes for our vocabulary test. After school on the thirty minute car ride, I will listen to my audio book on law again. Once I get home I will spend thrity minutes getting my food, clothes and work materils ready. I will spend forty-five minutes working on the last two pages of my paper. After I will spend fifteen minutes on social media. In the ten-minute car ride to work, I will relax by listening to my two favorite songs. On the ride home I will talk to my friend. Once I'm home I will Facetime my friend for ten minutes. Then I'll spend forty-five minutes showering, eating dinner and preparing for bed.

The last three examples should have woke up that little inner voice in your head. Right now you two are in agreement: the Great category from the value chart is more challenging.

You're not sure if you want it that badly. To reach the success you want from this life, you will have to pay for it, in full, daily. Now is the best time to attack your value chart. Blocking out strategically with hours first will make you more productive. As you see the results try to move towards the Great practice of smaller blocks.

This chart is not soley focused on income but more on outcomes.

The more detailed a person is with their twenty-four hours, the less anxious and frustrated they become. There will be more gaps for fun as you detail your twenty-four hours.

Maybe this will help:

Visualize a father trying to fly to his sick child's bedside across the United States as the child's health is fading away. As the father is about to board the connecting flight that will have him in the city in forty-five minutes, he hears there will be an hour delay until the flight takes off.

The father arrives and takes an Uber ride to the hospital. In a matter of a few minutes, the father is taking the elevator to the child's floor. But seconds prior to reaching the bedside, his child took his last breath.

Pause and internalize that feeling for forty-five seconds.

Yes, time is the most precious commodity you have been afforded, and most people don't truly value every second of it until it's life or death: a make or break moment vs. time.

Now revisit the story and ask yourself how much do you believe the father would have paid to take a flight hours earlier, just to ensure that he could have those last minutes with his child? To remember being there in the seconds before the last breath, holding the child's hand?

If you said all the money in the father's bank account, I agree because, being a father myself and faced with that choice, I would pay it all for one extra second. This is the mindset possessed by peak performers in this world. They see the value of second as life or death to their goals and dreams daily.

How do they develop such a value on time? Usually, they have been in a situation wherein each second mattered. Take for instance arguably the greatest NBA basketball player ever, Michael Jordan, who made a total of twenty-five game-winning shots in his career. Eight of those shots were at the buzzer, meaning there was barely a full second up on the clock or less. Talk about valuing time! Jordan also missed twenty-six game-winning shots, but he had the urgency to at least shoot the total fifty-one attempts at his dreams. The truth is you don't have to make every shot or goal you chase, but if you lack the time to shoot for it, then you already took the *L.*

Now have a look at two geniuses from world history and their strategic schedules. These will definitely teach us a thing or two about how to make the most of each twenty-four hours. We can definitely take inspiration from them.

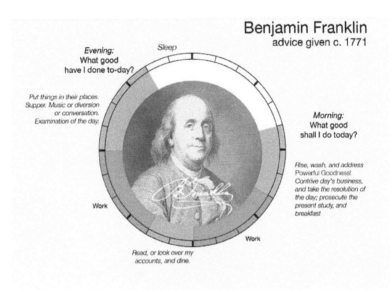

Benjamin Franklin
advice given c. 1771

Evening:
What good
have I done to-day?

Sleep

Put things in their places.
Supper. Music or diversion
or conversation.
Examination of the day.

Morning:
What good
shall I do today?

Rise, wash, and address
Powerful Goodness!
Contrive day's business,
and take the resolution of
the day; prosecute the
present study, and
breakfast

Work

Work

Read, or look over my
accounts, and dine.

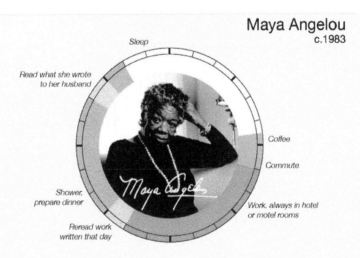

Maya Angelou
c.1983

Sleep

Read what she wrote
to her husband

Coffee

Commute

Shower,
prepare dinner

Work, always in hotel
or motel rooms

Reread work
written that day

What would your schedule look like?

(IndiaTimes.com Lifestyle)

"A MAN WHO DARES TO WASTE ONE HOUR OF LIFE HAS NOT DISCOVERED THE VALUE OF LIFE." —CHARLES DARWIN

The first step is to evaluate dead time.

Yes, the hours, minutes and seconds you spend not pursuing your dreams passionately or doing productive neccassary work are deemed "DEAD TIME."

It is said that misery loves company but so does the dead time. For example, the time spent on the phone, electronics, hanging out, and of course oversleeping.

Let's start at the ringing of your morning alarm clock. That piercing noise begins, and you know what time it is.

What is your reaction to killing a few more minutes with sleep, the cousin of death? Do you reach for the snooze button, or do you wake that passion up and take advantage of the first second of your day?

More than half of Americans are snoozers, according to a study by French tech firm Withings, with results showing we spend a total of 3.5 months of our lives hitting the snooze button. The company conducted the same survey in the UK, which showed that Brits have even more difficulties waking up, with seventy percent admitting to regularly hitting snooze.

Additionally, 58% of the Americans admit to staying in bed for more than five minutes every morning, while 64% of Brits do. This equates to Americans individually spending nearly two days a year, or 577 million days for the nation as a whole snoozing.

In the study, 57% of Americans reported still feeling tired after a night's sleep, and only 33% defining their wake up experience as good. The study found total sleep time per person to be six hours and forty-eight minutes per night.

—*sleepreviewmag.com 2014-08*

Now it's time to assess why you're not where you should be at this stage of your life. No matter your age or gender, you're now proven guilty of killing your valuable gift: time.

Let's take a close look at a few people in history who refused to have dead time.

"How wonderful it is that nobody need wait a single moment before starting to improve the world." —Anne Frank

During the Holocaust, at the age of thirteen, Anne Frank began writing in her diary. In an intense, cruel environment, it had to be very difficult to sleep at all, let alone snooze. Because of her commitment to her writing time during those two years in hiding, she left her mark on the world forever. Sometimes it takes a person facing huge odds to maximize their time. Despite her short life, she reached her goal of becoming an author. Anne Frank definetly used her time efficiently to write and leave her mark on this world in her final years.

"The time is always right to do what is right."
— Dr. Martin Luther King Jr.

Dr. King is another example of someone with a short life who, however, decided not to have a ton of dead time. Though his name rarely enters into discussions on the art of time management, Dr. King was like Pablo Picasso to the craft.

We often forget that the ultimate aim of time management is to improve one's capacity to accomplish what one aims to accomplish. It's not about meticulously maintaining lists. It's not about perfectly organizing documents. It's not about efficiently plugging away at important tasks every second of the day.

Time management is about setting your sights on what you want and following through until either you achieve what you set out to achieve or decide it's no longer worthwhile. At this, Dr. King was unmatched.

—forbes.com/sites patbrans 2013-01-18

At the age of just fifteen, he graduated from high school. By the age of twenty-six, he earned his doctorate degree. In his thirty-nine years, he accomplished so much, including winning a Nobel Peace Prize and numerous other distinguished awards. He led nonviolent marches that helped to transform the American culture and gave way to many of the first levels of integration. With a resume like that it would be impossible to imagine Dr. King hitting the snooze button.

"Making the most of your time, because the days are evil." —Ephesians 5:16

One of the most famous people to ever walk the Earth even has a time period named after him because of his lack of dead time. At the age of only thirty-three, He was killed. The life refered to is the life of Jesus Christ. No matter your religious beliefs, there is a time frame called B.C. which in Latin means before Christ and A.D. which means the year of the Lord. His work has lived for thousands of years. He left his mark on the world as well. According to his followers called disciples, Jesus would often sacrifice sleep to accomplish His goals during those thirty-three years.

How do you begin to move from having a substantial amount of dead time to leaving your mark with efficient alive time? How do you shake the desire to join those who press the snooze button? How can you regain two full days a year?

It's time for a visual plan to strengthen your will, to find that level of importance required to get up and after your day immediately.

Step 1: Create a time chart similar to the one below.

Step 2: Create a chart breaking down a normal day.

Step 3: Begin the process of taking thirty minutes of time from sleep time.

Step 4: After taking the time, allot it the most important of the other three categories.

Step 5: Next, begin to implement the 7-by-7 Rule. If it won't matter in seven years, don't waste more than seven minutes on it.

How I use my time **WILL** change:

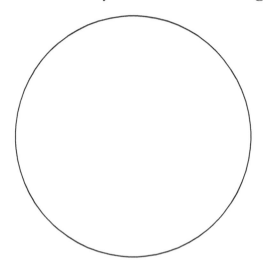

My goals for my 168 hour week are:

Sleep: _____

Eating, Travel, Family Time: _____

Work: _____

School: _____

Pursuing My Dreams: _____

BUM VERSUS BILLIONAIRE

Both get twenty-four hours in a day. Which one's time management are you closer to?

It's the value in each second, minute and hour that allows one to become and the other to succumb. Build your schedule wisely and edit it often.

After five weeks, reevaluate your chart and make the necessary changes. The little changes make the biggest differences over time.

Reevaluated Use of Time:

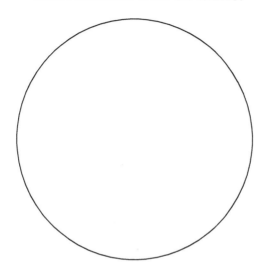

My goals for my 168 hour week are:

Sleep: _____
Eating, Travel, Family Time: _____
Work: _____
School: _____
Pursuing My Dreams: _____

3 ROUTINE

" It's not enough to be busy, so are the ants. The question is, what are we busy about?" —Henry David Thoreau

What's the secret of the world's most successful people?

They started in the same conditions as you and me or in many cases worse. Their day holds as many hours as yours or mine. And they surely don't have superhuman strength or energy. What is it then that separates them from you and me—and how can you close that gap? The answer is daily routines.

—developgoodhabits.com

This is the birthing process to dominate your time. Unlike a mother waiting to give birth, it won't take nine months to birth a healthy routine. However, it will share some of the pains and lack of sleep at times. But the results are as satisfying as that of a mother holding her child for the first time.

A healthy routine, if attacked daily for 21-66 days, will become almost automatic. Yes, it will be uncomfortable at first, but don't allow your feelings to deny your ability to be successful.

The ability to master your first five is essential to creating a productive routine. In the previous chapter we focused on not hitting the snooze button. Now what? This is where having a definite purpose will carry a person from their bed to the first important task.

Here is a personal example of how I start and end my day.

"You can't beg borrow or buy any more time today." —J.R. Rivera

So, for me, as a former professional athlete, my routine is to tap into my mind, body, and soul every morning.

My routine is five hundred push-ups every morning Monday through Sunday. If the day happens, the push-ups happen. But the most important thing is my *Why*, my purpose for doing them. It's not to have an amazing physique but rather to challenge my mind and body never to give up when times become challenging from the start of my day. While I'm doing the push-ups, I'm visualizing my goals and thanking the creator.

In my daily routine, I cheat time by completing complementary tasks together. This multi-tasking allows me to have more time to do other things in the morning. I also listen to audio books as I drive so that I can read as I travel. The more I can do at once, the more the time I can spend pursuing my dreams.

I don't set all my clocks back during daylight savings time to gain an hour of life. I try to arrive early everywhere. That is important to get the full experiences. I have had conversations only lasting one minute that changed my life, so I value all sixty seconds.

At the closing of my day, I use a method I learned listening to the great Napoleon Hill. My last deep thought before bed activates my subconscious to keep working on my dreams while I sleep. Warning: This has caused me to wake up at odd hours in the early morning to write down ideas and speeches quickly. I call it "working on the dream while you dream."

When two of the wealthiest men in the world, Warren Buffett and Bill Gates, met for the first time, a question arose: **What was the most important ingredient to their success?**

Of course they both had an answer.

Bill wanted to go first. But so did Warren.

Simultaneously, they opened their mouths and said: *"My focus. My laser focus is the reason for my enormous wealth."*

Think about it. A habit is, by definition, an automatic behavior. It frees your mind from having to think. The more good habits you develop, the more time and energy you have left to spend on moving forward with important things.

So what Bill and Warren really meant when they said *focus* are the habits they acquired to create a daily routine that maximizes their time and energy to focus on important aspects of their business.

You can take a few steps toward creating your own daily routine simply by developing a few meta-habits, habits that help you form habits.

For example: If you want to work ten hours a day, which is a lot, and be productive at the same time, you could jump right into working ten hours a day and probably fail after a week.

By using meta-habits, you would first **create the habits that enable you to work ten hours a day**, and then pick up the actual habit.

That could be habits like sleeping nine hours per night, eating at least 2,000 calories each day, exercising every day, taking a walk each evening, and so on, to make sure you actually have the energy to work that much.

Here are seven good meta-habits to help you create a daily routine that you can repeat day in and day out. This way, you too can maximize focusing on important work to become successful, no matter how you personally define success.

Meta-Habit 1: Track your current habits.

"Know thyself" is an old, Greek aphorism, used by many Stoic prophets to express that progress always follows observation. In order to make improvements in your daily routine and see which habits work well for you, and which don't, you must first track your habits.

This comes in two phases: taking stock of your current habits and then continuously monitoring current and future habits that you want to develop.

Phase 1: To take stock of all of your current habits, write down what a typical day looks like for you with times.

Here's an example:

Morning activities:
- wake up – 5 am
- check phone (emails, twitter)
- shower – 5:30 am
- breakfast – 5:45 am
- check social media
- leave for school or work – 6 am

Get home from school or work:
- go to gym – 4 pm
- work out (weights or cardio)
- leave gym and drive home – 5 pm
- shower and dinner – 6:30 pm
- watch TV – 7:30 pm
- sleep – 10 pm

List and mark your **good habits** and *bad habits.*

Meta-Habit 2: Use a calendar.

Everyone has a calendar. The question is are you actually using yours the right way? Modern calendars are overloaded with functions no one needs. All the reminders, invitations, location-functions and URL attachments are nice and they can be useful.

Yet the ancient Romans didn't expect any of those when they came up with the word *calendarium*, which meant register.

Remember that. A calendar is meant for you to register and keep track of appointments and commitments.

We often think successful people never have time because they're always busy working. This is not true.

They fiercely protect their time.

Instead of just putting appointments with other people in your calendar, **create appointments with yourself and map out all of your time.** Block several hours at once to get big chunks of work done and be sure to set a start and end point for your daily routine.

For example, if you want to become an athlete, be sure to schedule practice and workouts early in the morning and also set a block at night to review your workouts and practices. Also use that time to plan workouts for the next day.

Meta-Habit 3: Set an alarm in the morning AND at night.

A good daily routine hinges on it's beginning and end points. Your routine doesn't have to take up the entire day, just a part of it.

But if you don't mark the start and end of it, it will never happen.

Your morning alarm can mark the time of your waking up and the start of your morning routine, if you choose to have one, but it could also be set a little later, to mark the start of your actual school or work day.

For example, if you want to give yourself a buffer between 6–7 am before starting school or work, set an alarm not only when you want to wake up but also at 7 am.

The alarm at night serves as a trigger to wrap up your day and start to wind down.

I know from personal experience that it's easy to get worked up and want to work longer at night just because you're on a roll. However, that often results in neglecting other important areas of your life.

Recognize you are protecting yourself from exhaustion and a lack of preparation for the next day. You are better off with a proper evening routine that gives your brain and body a chance to calm down and also helps you set yourself up for a successful tomorrow.

—*developgoodhabits.com/daily-routine-success/*

Those three meta-habits will be the foundation, the key to creating morning and evening routines. Highly successful people don't necessarily work themselves to the bone, obsessing about every detail of their business.

Fun fact: according to interviews Warren Buffet is said to spend his first five hours of his day reading. It makes up 80% of his daily routine. He's not on the computer or his phone, and he doesn't have meetings.

In conclusion the value of foundation is revealed when it's time to carry the heavy daily load. So in this next challenge, you will be given the summarized steps to create a solid foundation.

Cheating Time Challenge:

1- Set your morning alarm or wake up time ten minutes earlier.
2- Value those ten minutes as earned champion time.
3- For two of those minutes, only say the most positive ten things you believe you could be: "I AM" thankful, motivated, full of energy, focused, healthy, etc.
4- Do a light three minute exercise: for example push-ups, jumping jacks or jogging in place.
5- Stretch for three minutes with your eyes closed, visualizing yourself in your dream house.
6- Activate all five senses with your dream for two minutes: hear it, see it, smell it, taste it, and, soon, you will touch it.
7- Now it's time to attack life.

Use this space to record your day from the time you rise from bed.

Task	Time
Feet hit the ground	
2 mins. (I AM)	
3 mins. Exercise	
3 mins. Visualize & Stretch (Eyes closed)	
2 mins. Activate 5 senses	

How do you feel after completing this routine the first time?

_____

_____

_____

After the twenty-first day?

_____

_____

_____

4 TIME INVESTMENT

"The key is in not spending time, but in investing it." —Stephen R. Covey

Consider these questions: Who and where are you supposed to be by now? How many life changing moments have you already slept through?

Personally, I would have to argue that I have missed my fair share of such moments, and I'm fed up with missing out. How about you?

With that being said, what is the value you have on your time?

This leads me to share this famous thought with you from T.D. Jakes' *Destiny*.

"Imagine there is a bank account that credits your account each morning with $86,400. It carries over no balance from day to day. Every evening the bank deletes whatever part of the balance you failed to use during the day. What would you do? Draw out every cent, of course. Each of us has such a bank, its name is time. Every morning, it credits you with 86,400 seconds. Every night it writes off at a loss, whatever of this you failed to invest to a good purpose. It carries over no balance. It allows no overdraft. Each day it opens a new account for you. Each night it burns the remains of the day. If you fail to use the day's deposits, the loss is yours. There is no drawing against "tomorrow." You must live in the present on today's deposits. Invest it so as to get from it the utmost in health, happiness, and wealth. The clock is running. Make the most of today."

— Marc Levy

Instead of asking how much time you're wasting each day, ask how much money you're wasting each day. That perspective alone should transform your focus level and help you invest your time better daily. Imagine how much of the gap can be made up from that mindset.

Fun fact: CEO Indra Nooyi's approaches to managing PepsiCo can also be applied to investing in time management. Balance your short-term objectives with your long-term goals. One must look at the things that pay off in the short run and balance the time on those items with others that have longer-term returns.

CEO Jeff Immelt of General Electric told *Fortune* magazine that "There are twenty-four hours in a day, and you can use all of them."

CEO of Twitter and payment-processing specialist Square Jack Dorsey has a unique method of assigning a theme for each day that allows him to more accurately invest time into each company.

Pat Gelsinger became CEO of VMW in 2012 after a successful career serving in executive roles with several other technology companies. He told the *Wall Street Journal* in

2014 that he invests in color-codeing every minute of his day on his schedule. Different colors are used for different activities, such as turquoise for meetings with customers and yellow for strategy review. Gelsinger has an intern later analyze how his investment of time compares with studies that have been done on executive time management.

Those are a few examples of amazingly successful CEO's who know they must invest in time management before stocks or any other business moves can be made.

—http://host.madison.com/business/investment/markets-and-stocks/time-management-secrets

Can you buy more time?

The answer is no. You're always losing time but you can't find or buy more.

However you can get more usefulness from the investments you make through wise time management strategies. They will alter the quality of your hours each day.

For example, I once was driving one hour to work and another hour to return from work. That's twice a day for five days per week. I can never get back those ten hours.

So I began to make use of those hours. I invested in them by listening to audio books that focused on my career path. I was able to revive my reading time, which I had lost to the communte.

I then became a father and wanted more time with my son. So I invested in higher rent to be thirty-five minutes closer to my job, which meant I stretched my time with my son by those thirty-five minutes a day. At that time I also allotted myself a few more minutes to rest and start my daily routine each morning.

Right now, I dare you to pause from this reading and grab a pen and start writing down as many areas in your life as you can think of that could be stretched for more quality hours. Remember, it may take a financial investment or a risk in other areas.

Steward Time

" Take care of the minutes, and the hours will take care of you." —J.R. Rivera

Set aside a block of time to invest in and affirm others. This means that you need to sow an unreplenishable resource to someone who can't afford it. I can't explain how important this one is. For some reason beyond my understanding, the world seems to pay you back in a breakthrough way.

You get breaks that you could not have earned through work in twenty years. You get favor in areas you could not pay for like family, finances, and opportunities. So, in turn, you save time by investing in others.

"Someone is sitting in the shade today because someone planted a tree a long time ago."
—Warren Buffet

Name 3 people you can invest in and when.

Name	Day you will invest
1.	
2.	
3.	

How do you feel after investing in person 1?

_____

_____.

How do you feel after investing in person 2?

_____

_____.

How do you feel after investing in person 3?

_____

_____.

How has that impacted your time?

_____.

5 PROTECT YOUR TIME

"Never let yesterday use up today."
—Richard H. Nelson

You cannot continue to spend unaccounted time with everyone, or you begin to create vulnerability within your time to make your dreams a reality.

Show me your calendar, and I'll show you your priorities.

If your life is constantly in a reactive state and you live exclusively for others, your tank will run dry. You will feel exhausted, overwhelmed and resentful. It is absolutely imperative that you carve out some of your time for yourself that cannot be comprimised.

How does that look in action?

Lots of front end sacrifices and more use of the word "no." If your not already missing out on some of the latest television series, movies and sporting events, get ready. One might be lead to believe you would be sacrificing lots of reletionships and time with others, and this is somewhat true.

However, the true sacrifice and protection will come with your personal distractions and entertainment.

Nowadays, with distraction being so convient and small we are able to carry it with us everywhere we go in a pocket, it is that much easier to be in the middle of an important task and decide to check our ever-so-time-consuming phone, social media, e-mails etc.

According to *Social Media Today*, the amount of time people spend on social media is constantly increasing. Teens and young adults now spend up to nine hours a day on social platforms, while thirty percent of all time spent online is now allocated to social media interaction. And the majority of that social media time is facilitated by a mobile device.

How does this translate into what could be done if that time were more guarded and protected?

Astonishingly, the average person will spend nearly two hours on social media everyday, which translates to a total of five years and four months spent over a lifetime. Even more, time spent on social is only expected to increase as platforms continue to develop, eating further into traditional media, most notably TV. Right now, the average person will spend seven years and eight months watching TV in a lifetime. However, as digital media consumption continues to grow at unprecedented rates, this number is expected to shrink in counter to that expansion.

Currently, total time spent on social media beats time spent eating and drinking, socializing and grooming.

Broken down, time spent on social media differs across each platform. YouTube comes in first, consuming over forty minutes of a person's day or one year and ten months in a lifetime. Users of Facebook and its subsidies will spend an average of thirty-five minutes a day, totalling one year and seven months in a lifetime. Snapchat and Instagram come in next with twenty-five minutes and fifteen minutes spent per day, respectively. Finally, users will spend one minute on Twitter. That single minute will span eighteen days of usage over a lifetime.

What can you accomplish in five years and four months during the course of your life span?

Fly to the moon and back a total of thirty-two times. How about walk the entire Great Wall Of China a total of three and a half times. If that's not impressive enough, one could climb to the top of mount Everest thirty times. You could run in over ten thousand marathons or walk your dog ninety-three thousand times.

So no matter how far fetched and high you have your goals, they are well attainable if you can protect even half or a third of that social media time and put it to use climbing the task that leads to your dreams and goals.

If those statistics don't have you seeing your dreams as possible here is another story of how protecting your time can lead you further and faster down the path of success.

Highly successful millionaire FloRida once told me a story of how he protected his time and dreams earlier on. While standing around in his recording studio in Miami, I asked Flo what helped him early on in his start up as a rapper and business genius? Flo said that he never told anyone in high school that he could rap or where he was going after school to spend his time. All the while, he was putting in countless hours perfecting his craft in the studios. This protected not only his time from being manipulated by friends and family memebers with tasks they deemed as important or more worthy of his time. Also this protected him from critics with no credentials, and instead gave him time to nurture his gift.

When he told me this, it immediately brought to mind an African proverb: If you understand the beginning well, the end will not trouble you.

It's the start of how you protect your time that will help solidify your destination point.

Now is the time to identify who or what is eating up your time. Develop a solid protection plan over twenty-one days using the previous charts and challenges to guide you. There is no one size that fits all, but we can adjust the size to fit our goals.

"Every time you say 'yes' to spending time on something, you are inevitably saying 'no' to spending time on something else."
—J.R. Rivera

Challenge:

Write down 2 new ways you can protect your time.

I will protect my time by:

_____

and:

_____.

Take a look at them once a day for 21 days.

I have protected my time by:

_____

and:

_____.

6 WINNING THE BATTLE

"Whether it's the best of times or the worst of times, it's the only time we've got."
—Art Buchwald

Time and your goals are in a constant battle.

Before a competitor engages in a competition, it behooves one to practice and stretch for maximum results. So winning against time requires the same. There must be a plan. Treat each week like the biggest championship you will ever be in.

Dare to be CHAMPIONS!

- C – Courage to get up early.
- H – Honor your hourly commitments
- A – Attitude of gratitude for each second
- M – Motivation to keep pursing the daily goal
- P – Perseverance to out last the distractions
- I – Integrity of being fully in the moment
- O – Optimism knowing it will be worth it
- N – Never Give Up.

Champions dominate their practice time so on gameday they're well prepared. Time management requires its own practice time as well. The first twenty one days trying to establish a well-thoughtout routine that maximizes each block of time will prepare you for the bigger moments life offers. It will take effort and laser focus to dominate your time management plans. The goal is to get one percent better each day. Pick out a block of time you are wasting on distractions. Next practice taking small bits of that time and putting it to use for school, writing, excercising, practicing a skill or reading. Even with five "practice" minutes of reading everyday for a month, you will have read for one hundred fifty minutes. Or imagine if you were to practice fifteen minutes a day for a month; that would be four hundred fifty practice minutes. I guarantee that amount of applied practice will better your life substancially.

Practice does not make perfect but enough of it does make a habit permenant.

Practice accounting for your time usage for a day, then a week, and then a month. Practice executing the details in seconds.

Practice doing more with less time. Warning: This is a learned skill that takes—you guessed it—time. This is what seperates champion weeks from status-quo, mundane weeks.

Remember, it is natural for humans to enjoy working, but we also feel pleased to waste time on any kind of entertainment. Thus, we have to battle against our laziness and organize our schedule in such a fashion that we prepare to win.

So I start from creating a to-do list. I list all the things I have to do and sort them by date according to importance and urgency. Also I put entries into groups such as daily life, work and the dream. At the end of day, I cross all the things I have finished. When I see the crossings, it really makes me feel a sense of achievement.

Time management is not hard to learn, and from my experience, you can tell that success comes easily with a well-organized schedule.

The challenge is planning an escape from the strong grip of distractions wrapped around each secound of our everyday lives. It's like you're in a heavy weight fight: you don't fight for twelve rounds without any breaks. However you time the breaks just like the breaks in the competitons are timed. Schedule your breaks during your battle, allotting time each day. Then, once that alarm goes off to start back working, go in with everything you have.

You can also easy your mind knowing that, like a heavy weight fight, you don't have to win every round every day, but the more you win the better the payoff.

Imagine a life where your time did not dictate where you had to be but where you chose to be. That is what I call a successful battle against time, my friend.

Challenge Time:

Use more than you lose daily.

1. Calculate your gains and losses

Sleep can be a gain or a loss depending on its necessity.

Gains	Losses
Reading 1hr.	Social Media 1hr.
Working Out 45 mins.	Video Games 45mins.
Rest 1hr.	Bored Naps 1hr.

The gains are the necessary things that help you on the path to success. Losses are distractions that distance you from reaching goals.

2. The goal is to have more gains than losses each day. Stop taking "L's."

Are you going to fight or lose the battle?

When is it and how do you prepare for it?

This fight starts from the moment we enter the world: it's you versus time. The experienced veteran of Father Time versus a newborn sounds very unfair, right?

That's life, an unfair bully looking to make you tapout and quit.

In an effort to thoroughly produce a sense of urgency, imagine birthdays that subtract instead of add a year to your age.

You start the countdown from the day you're born at a hundred years old. After your first year, happy 99th birthday, baby. Once have reached a normal thirty years of life, you would have counted down to seventy years. The reality of your time going down is like a basketball player trying to make a game winner with time expiring. There's pressure, but the greats embrace it and take the shot.

Of course, with this rationale, the question is raised: What would happen if you lived past a hundred years? It is simple, you have outlived your time and entered bonus years. Everyone loves a good bonus round!

Next comes the battle against the pits of procrastination. Procrastination is the pit we all unenjoyably fall into. The key is to get out as quickly as possible.

The best way to get out of a pit is to stop digging. What I'm saying is that in my own experience, I have been my own worst enemy in the pit. The more I dug in, the further I strayed from my goal. The moment I stopped digging, I began to find a way out.

You see we are wired as problem solvers, and the more we use this skill, the less time we waste with each problem.

I use a pause method to regain my focus. I call it a focus alarm. Set it for the time that you seem to get stuck procrastinating the most on a normal day. As you narrow down the hours you need to gain back from the battle pits of procrastination, you will stop the digging and begin to find a way out of the hole.

Challenge

1. Stop counting down until Friday or the next vacation or the next weekend and then living miserable all the other days.

   Favorite   day   of   the   week:

   _____

2. Listen to a song that makes you feel like its Friday if you love the feeling. (Flo Rida "Hello Friday")

   Song name: _____

   _____

7 TICKS

"One thing you cannot recycle is a wasted second, minute or hour." —J.R. Rivera

Clocks tick, but so does a bomb. Your life is on a countdown. You can blow up and become a success or blow up so you're left with nothing.

"Tick, tick, tick!" the clock moved, but did you move toward your goal? The ticks of time can inconvenience you or inspire you.

Here is the burning question: How many ticks will it take for you to take off?

3, 2, 1.... Go for it!

You now possess the tools to strategieze stretching each minute. The plan is strategically all mapped out at this point. Navigate your way to having the time to live the life you dream of living.

Ponder these questions:

Where will your new time management tools and knowledge lead you? To financial freedom? Your own business? A professional athletic career? A happy family?

This was a lot, so let's summarize the 7 meta-habits that will help you form your own daily routine for success:

Meta-Habit 1: Take stock of your current habits by writing down your typical day. Then continuously monitor all of them.

Meta-Habit 2: Use a calendar to schedule appointments with yourself and map out the use of all your time.

Meta-Habit 3: Set an alarm both in the morning and at night to mark the start and end of your daily routine.

Meta-Habit 4: Create a morning routine to lead yourself right into the school or work part of your daily routine.

Meta-Habit 5: Remember to stick to an evening routine to set yourself up for a successful next day.

Meta-Habit 6: Early on treat weekends like weekdays to really make your routine stick long-term.

Meta-Habit 7: Track your time in structured blocks to make sure you're using your strengths as much as possible.

What will your daily routine look like?
What will you use these meta-habits for?

BONUS QUOTES

"Mastery of time is the mother that births a purposeful life." —J.R. Rivera

"Everyone wants to live a long time, but no one wants to be old." —Baki

"For every minute you are angry, you lose sixty seconds of joy."
—Ralph Waldo Emerson

"How do you afford a million-dollar dream? You pay it in full with quality time."
—J.R. Rivera

"The two most powerful warriors are patience and time." —Leo Tolstoy

"Time is the coin of your life. You spend it. Do not allow others to spend it for you."
—Carl Sandburg

"Don't live the same year seventy-five times and call it a life." —Robin S. Sharma

"Time is either trying to run us over or pass us by." —J.R. Rivera

I encourage the use of the free resources I have provided to motivate you to master the time you are given.

Daily motivation on Instagram @_jrrivera
On twitter @rivera_reachesu

You can book me to speak at your event at milemindset.com

The time to be the best you is now!

#Mile

ABOUT THE AUTHOR

J.R. Rivera inspires and motivates across the country for the Mile Mindset LLC and consults with educational programs, universities, athletes, business and churches. He has spoken on BET Networks, numerous talk shows, radio programs, and events for governors, and mayors. He resides in Florida.